Yum! ¡MmMm! ¡Qué Rico!

Americas' Sproutings

Haiku by Pat Mora

Pictures by Rafael López

LEE & LOW BOOKS INC.

NEW YORK

la cocina: kitchen
los dulces: sweets, candy
la luna: moon
qué rico: delicious

Acknowledgments

I'm grateful to my husband, professor of anthropology Vern Scarborough, who
teaches a course on the Origins of Agriculture and was a helpful and enthusiastic resource;
and to author, conservationist, and ethno-botanist Gary Paul Nabhan, for his
helpful and inspiring books and for his energetic example. —*P.M.*

Author's Sources

Coe, Sophie. *America's First Cuisines.* Austin: University of Texas Press, 1994.
Foster, Nelson, and Linda S. Cordell. *Chiles to Chocolate: Food the Americas Gave
the World.* Tucson: University of Arizona Press, 1996.
Nabhan, Gary Paul. *Gathering the Desert.* Tucson: University of Arizona Press, 1985.

I have consulted numerous other books, dictionaries, and Internet sources in exploring the
origins of foods and words included in this book. On some topics there is general consensus;
on others, varying sources propose different theories. Linguists and botanists continue
to discuss and investigate these etymologies and indigenous plant histories. —*P.M.*

Text copyright © 2007 by Pat Mora
Illustrations copyright © 2007 by Rafael López
All rights reserved. No part of this book may be reproduced, transmitted,
or stored in an information retrieval system in any form or by any means,
electronic, mechanical, photocopying, recording, or otherwise, without
written permission from the publisher.
LEE & LOW BOOKS Inc., 95 Madison Avenue, New York, NY 10016
leeandlow.com
Manufactured in China by Jade Productions, March 2014
Book design by Christy Hale
Book production by The Kids at Our House
The text is set in Egyptian 505 and Mex Regular
The illustrations are rendered in acrylic on wood panels
HC 10 9 8 7 6 5
PB 10 9 8 7 6 5 4 3 2
First Edition
Library of Congress Cataloging-in-Publication Data
Mora, Pat.
Yum! ¡mmmm! ¡qué rico! : Americas' sproutings / haiku by Pat Mora ;
pictures by Rafael López. — 1st ed.
p. cm.
Summary: "From blueberries to vanilla, indigenous foods of the Americas
are celebrated in this collection of haiku, which also includes
information about each food's origins"—Provided by publisher.
ISBN 978-1-58430-271-1 (HC)   ISBN 978-1-60060-892-6 (PB)
1. Food—Poetry. 2. Fruit—America—Poetry. 3. Vegetables—America—Poetry.
4. Fruit—America. 5. Vegetables—America. I. López, Rafael. II. Title.
PN6110.F73M67 2007
811'.54—dc22   2006038199

To Chris Hazard,
a wonderful friend, cook,
and fellow food lover
—P.M.

For my mother Pillo
blooming in her *cocina*
aromatic poems of love
—R.L.

N

W E

S

Blueberries are delicious, healthy treats. Originating in North America, they were eaten fresh and dried by Native Americans. They also ground blueberries into spice rubs and used the berries in medicines. European settlers in North America made gray paint by boiling blueberries in milk, and today the United States is the largest producer of blueberries in the world. Wild blueberries, the official state berry of Maine, are sometimes harvested using traditional handheld rakes. Plan a blueberry party in July, National Blueberry Month.

BLUEBERRY

Fill your mouth with blue.

Share a bowl heaped with summer.

Chew indigo O.

Chile peppers probably began their world journey in Mexico and are still used as a favorite spice and seasoning throughout the Americas. Called *chilli* in Nahuatl, the language of the Aztecs and one of the original languages of Mexico, the word became *chile* in Spanish and *chili* in English. *Chiles* come in a variety of shapes and colors and range from mild to extremely hot. Because the heat in *chiles* makes us perspire, *chiles* are like an internal air conditioner. After they make us feel hot, they cool us off.

CHILE

Dad bites green mouth-fire,
laughs when tears fill his eyes, sighs,
"¡Mmmm! This heat tastes good."

Chocolate is native to Central or South America, although the exact origin of this popular food is often debated. Chocolate is made from the seeds in the pods of the tropical cacao tree. The word *chocolate* comes from the Nahuatl word *xocolatl*, which means "bitter water." The Aztecs roasted cacao seeds, ground them, and mixed them with water and seasonings to make a spicy drink. The pods were so highly prized, they were even used as money. Yes, money grew on trees!

CHOCOLATE

Fudge, cake, pie, cookies.
Brown magic melts on your tongue.
Happy, your eyes dance.

Corn, also called maize, is a member of the cereal family. Its ancient ancestor is a wild Mexican grass called *teosinte*, which means "God's corn." This wild corn was eventually domesticated and became a staple of many people's diets. Pueblo Indians of the southwestern United States planted corn of various colors, including blue; and corn is still offered in blessings at traditional Native American ceremonies. Today the starch from corn kernels is used as a binder to help crayons and chalk hold together.

CORN

Leaves sprout silk-snug house.
Smell grits, tortillas, corn bread.
Pass the butter, please.

Cranberries are tart fall fruits. They
may be native to Wisconsin, where about
half of the United States crop grows on
woody, trailing vines in sandy marshes
or bogs. The berries were used by Native
Americans for food, dyes, and medicines.
Some say they were called craneberries
because cranes liked to slosh through
the bogs looking for a bright red snack.
Others say they were called craneberries
because their pink spring flowers look
like a crane's head. These fruits were
also called bearberries and bounceberries.
Can you guess why?

CRANBERRY

Marsh-floating hard bead
simmers then POPS! in hot pot.
Scarlet fireworks.

Papayas, also known as tree melons, are believed to have originated in southern Mexico and Central America. Now they are grown throughout the tropical and subtropical areas of the world. Papayas are hollow, with small, wrinkled black seeds in the center. Papain, found in the milky fluid of unripe papayas, is used in several products, including meat tenderizers and some medicines. When ripe, the fruit is juicy and sweet. Shaped somewhat like a pear, a papaya can weigh as much as twenty pounds.

PAPAYA

Chewing your perfume,
we taste your leafy jungle.
Yum! Juicy tropics.

Peanuts, or groundnuts, are from
South America, possibly Peru or Brazil.
Peanuts are not really nuts. Like beans
and peas, they are legumes, plants that
absorb nitrogen and enrich the soil.
African American botanist and inventor
George Washington Carver developed
more than three hundred uses for
peanuts. In the United States, six hundred
million pounds of peanuts and seven
hundred million pounds of peanut butter
are eaten each year. In March, National
Peanut Month, enjoy nibbling peanuts
mixed with dried fruits.

PEANUT

Smear nutty butter,
then jelly. Gooey party,
my sandwich and me.

Pecans grow on large trees native to Texas and northern Mexico. The pecan is the state tree of Texas, and there are almost a million acres of pecan trees along the state's rivers and streams. French settlers in North America named this tasty nut *pacane*, which means "nut to be cracked with a rock." The nuts were originally harvested by throwing sticks into the trees, to knock the nuts to the ground. Pecan pie is a traditional southern U.S. dessert.

PECAN

We crack hard, brown shells,
family munching, story time,
crunchy taste of fall.

Pineapple is a tropical fruit that originated in Paraguay and southern Brazil. Today it is the leading fruit crop of Puerto Rico, although Hawaiian pineapples are also prized for their delicious flavor. Pineapples are bromeliads. They have stiff, overlapping, waxy leaves that catch and hold water. Called *piña* in Spanish, which means "pinecone," the pineapple has skin that indeed resembles a very large pinecone. Hotels and inns sometimes decorate with pineapple shapes because this fruit is a symbol of hospitality.

PINEAPPLE

A stiff, spiky hat
on thick prickly skin, inside
hide syrupy rings.

Potatoes are native to the Andean mountains of Peru, Bolivia, and Ecuador in South America. The Aymara Indians of Bolivia developed more than two hundred varieties of potatoes, and the Indians of Peru have more than two hundred names for their varieties. Known as *papas* in Spanish, potatoes are the world's fourth food staple, after wheat, corn, and rice. Potatoes are nutritious and can be red, purple, pink, yellow, and even striped. In 1995 potatoes became the first vegetable grown in outer space.

POTATO

Underground magic.
Peel brown bundle, mash, pile high.
Salt and pepper clouds.

Prickly pear cactus may have come from Mexico, although their exact origin is unknown. Native Americans of the southwestern United States ate raw, cooked, and dried prickly pears. The fleshy green pads, known as *nopales* in Spanish, are modified stems or branches, not leaves. They can be served as a vegetable, like green beans, once the needles and skin are carefully removed and the pads sliced. The red fruits, called *tunas* in Spanish, are tricky to harvest. They are used to make juice, jams, and candy.

PRICKLY PEAR

Red desert wonder.
Cactus fruit becomes syrup
and *dulces*. Surprise!

Pumpkins are native to Central America. They belong to the plant family that includes cucumbers, melons, and squash. The word *pumpkin* comes from the Greek word *pepon*, which means "large melon." Native Americans wove mats of dried pumpkin strips and roasted pumpkin slices to eat. Pumpkin was once believed to remove freckles and cure snakebites. The majority of pumpkins sold in the United States today are used for decorations, including Halloween jack-o'-lanterns. As of 2006, the largest pumpkin grown weighed 1,502 pounds!

PUMPKIN

Under round luna,
scattered tumblings down the rows,
autumn's orange face.

Tomatoes probably originated in Peru or Mexico. They are eaten as a vegetable, but they are technically fruits. In 1893 the United States Supreme Court ruled that since tomatoes were commonly used as a vegetable, they should be subject to the government's tax on imported vegetables. Once considered poisonous, tomatoes are now one of the world's most prized foods. They come in many colors, including red, yellow, orange, green, purple, and white. Can you imagine pizza without tomato sauce or tacos without tomato salsa?

TOMATO

Round roly-poly
squirts seedy, juicy splatter.
Red bursts in your mouth.

Vanilla, native to Mexico and other tropical areas of the Americas, comes from the fruit of a vine in the orchid family. The fruit is a long pod called a vanilla bean that is filled with tiny black seeds. The Totonac Indians of Mexico discovered how to process vanilla pods and used vanilla as perfume, flavoring, medicine, and insect repellant. Today the United States is the world's largest consumer of vanilla, mostly in foods and beverages. July is National Ice Cream Month. The most popular flavor? Vanilla, of course!

VANILLA

Quick! Lick white river
running down the cone cooling
your warm summer laugh.

Dear Reader,

Let's gather all these good foods into a fast-clapping or jump-rope rhyme.

Blueberries, cranberries, prickly pear fiesta,
Tomatoes, chile, corn; spicy, spicy salsa.
Lime for papaya, cream for pumpkin, butter for potato.
Yum! Vanilla! Peanuts! Chocolate. ¡Mmmm! ¡Qué rico!

I love variety, don't you? I enjoy pansies and roses, parrots and doves, kittens and elephants, apples and cheese, Spanish and English. I like diversity in people and poetry too. I've so enjoyed writing my first book of haiku, those wonderful seventeen-syllable poems of Japanese origin. Haiku invite us to leap from image to image. Since I've also wanted to write a poetry collection about the native foods of the Americas, I combined these interests into this book of haiku about the foods that first sprouted here, before the Americas were divided into countries.

Scientists still debate the exact origins of plants such as blueberries, corn, cacao trees, and prickly pears. We do know that all these plants were grown and enjoyed by the peoples of the Americas long before Christopher Columbus or any other Europeans had ever tasted such wonderful foods. The world's variety is amazing—and delicious.

Pat Mora